Fife Council Education Department
King's Road Primary School
King's Crescent, Rosyth KY11 2RS

What is it like now...?

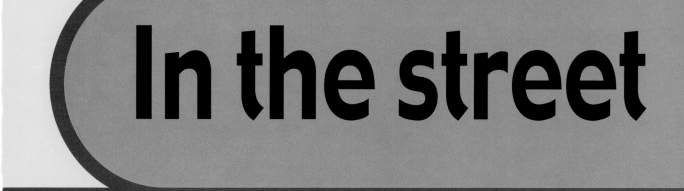

In the street

Heinemann
LIBRARY

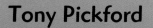

Tony Pickford

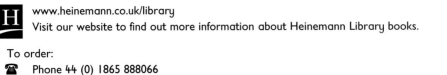

www.heinemann.co.uk/library
Visit our website to find out more information about Heinemann Library books.

To order:
☎ Phone 44 (0) 1865 888066
📄 Send a fax to 44 (0) 1865 314091
🖥 Visit the Heinemann Bookshop at www.heinemann.co.uk/library to browse our catalogue
and order online.

First published in Great Britain by Heinemann Library, Halley Court, Jordan Hill, Oxford OX2 8EJ,
a division of Reed Educational and Professional Publishing Ltd. Heinemann is a registered trademark
of Reed Educational & Professional Publishing Ltd.

OXFORD MELBOURNE AUCKLAND JOHANNESBURG BLANTYRE
GABORONE IBADAN PORTSMOUTH (NH) USA CHICAGO

Designed by Celia Floyd
Illustrations by Jo Brooker
Originated by Dot Gradations
Printed in Hong Kong/China

06 05 04 03 02
10 9 8 7 6 5 4 3 2 1
ISBN 0 431 15004 4

British Library Cataloguing in Publication Data
Pickford, Tony
What is it like in the street?
1. Streets – Juvenile literature
I. Title
388.4'11

Acknowledgements
The Publishers would like to thank the following for permission to reproduce photographs:
Ecoscene: Ian Harwood p24; Environmental Images: Toby Adamson p11, Steve Morgan p25
Photofusion: Bob Watkins pp26, 29; Travel Ink: p18, Dorothy Burrows p20; Sylvia Cordaiy Photo
Library: p21; Tudor Photography: p4, 5, 6, 7, 8, 9, 10, 12, 13, 14, 15, 16, 17, 22, 23, 27.

Cover photograph reproduced with permission of Getty.

Every effort has been made to contact copyright holders of any material reproduced in this book.
Any omissions will be rectified in subsequent printings if notice is given to the Publisher.

Contents

Words printed in **bold letters like these** are explained in the Glossary.

What is a street?

In every city, town and village there are streets. Down the middle of a street will be a road where **vehicles** go. The road is usually made of a hard, black **material** called tarmac.

Sometimes traffic is only allowed to go in one direction – this is called a one-way street. On either side of the road is a **pavement** where people can walk safely.

In this busy street there are pavements and a place in the middle for people to wait when crossing.

This is a quiet street where people live. Do you live in a street like this?

In parts of a town or city there will be streets with shops on either side. These shopping streets can be busy, noisy places. There are also quieter streets with houses on either side.

If you live in a street, what is it like? Is it very busy all day with lots of cars and people moving around? Or is it a quiet street with very little traffic?

A street of houses

In any one town there may be different types of streets. There are streets of **terraced** houses where the houses are in long rows on either side of the street. There are often cars parked on both sides of the road.

You need to be careful when crossing a street like this because the parked cars can block your view.

It is safe for children to play in this very quiet street.

In another part of town there are streets of **semi-detached** houses. The houses here have small gardens and places to park cars away from the road.

A street that does not lead to any other streets is called a cul-de-sac. Sometimes in the evening it is safe for children to play in this street because few cars are moving around.

What can you see in a street?

At the end of the street, there is usually a sign showing the name of the street. Sometimes a street might be called a Road, a Lane or a Drive. Do you know the name of your street?

A street name might give a clue about the area in the past. For example, Mill Street might be in a place where there was a windmill in the past.

This is Market Street — the name tells us that a market was held here in the past.

In most streets you will find lampposts. There will also be telephone wires that go from the houses to tall poles.

In the ground, metal covers allow workers to check and repair all the different pipes and **cables** that go into the houses. Look at the covers and you will see that they belong to gas, electricity, water and cable television companies.

This person is using a special machine to help him check and repair the lampposts in the street.

People in the street

Almost every day, streets are visited by people who do not live there. Early in the morning, milk will be delivered to some of the houses. A postman or woman will come to deliver letters.

Once a week, a big lorry will come to collect rubbish from the bins. Sometimes rubbish is put outside houses in plastic bags. In other streets the rubbish might be in wheelie bins.

This picture shows rubbish from a wheelie bin being put into the back of a special lorry.

On some days, people in the street might put out boxes and bags that hold bottles and newspapers for **recycling**. A special lorry comes around and workers collect the boxes and bags. Bottles and newspapers are taken to **factories** where they are used to make new bottles and sheets of paper.

People can leave their newspapers in a recycling box outside their house ready for collection.

In the countryside

There are also streets in **villages** in the countryside. The houses in the middle of a village might be **terraced** just like in towns and cities. Many houses will have gardens and will be more spread out than in a town. Sometimes there will be a farm near the middle of a village.

There are shops in this village street selling things to visitors and people who live in the village.

A village street can be almost as busy as one in a town on some days. People come to visit the village shop or to get stamps from the Post Office.

Just like in a town, letters and cards will be delivered in a village street and rubbish will be collected. On the edge of the village, the streets may be narrow with no **pavements** to walk on.

There is no pavement so these children are walking sensibly at the side of the road away from the traffic.

Around your street

What can you see around your street? In or near your street, you will find lots of things that you and your family find useful every day. There may be a postbox and local shops such as a newsagents or Post Office. Is there a park nearby where you and your friends can play?

Here are some local shops. Are there shops like these in or near your street?

There may be a crossing to help you get from one side of the road to the other. The crossing might have black and white markings on the road. This is called a **zebra crossing** and you must wait for **vehicles** to stop before you cross.

On other crossings there is a button to press. When you press this button, the traffic lights will change so that the traffic must stop to let you cross.

These children have pressed a button to change the traffic lights so they can cross the road safely.

Finding your way

There are some journeys that you do almost every day around the streets where you live. You go to school or to the shops or to the local swimming pool. You might walk there or go by car or bicycle. You will use the streets in different ways for different journeys – you might walk to school but go to the shops in a car.

A sign-post like this might help you to find your way around the streets.

Are there special buildings like these that you pass every day on your journeys?

Next time you go on a journey, try to spot objects in the street that you could use to find your way home. You could look for street signs or traffic signs.

You could look for a special building along the way such as a pub or a church. When you have finished your journey, make a list of the objects you have seen in the order that you saw them.

Your local area

The streets around your home and school are your local area. This is the place that you will know best because you travel along the streets every day.

There will be places where people work in your local area. As well as shops and schools, there might be offices or a **factory** or farms. Are there lots of trees in your local area?

Is your local area near the sea?

Make a map of your local area that shows all the places that you know. In the middle of your map will be your home and the street or road where you live. Around your home may be other roads where your friends might live. You could include your school and any open spaces in your local area, such as a park or playing field.

On your map draw all the interesting places in your local area.

Different local areas

What is your local area like? Do you live near the centre of a town? There will be many different buildings around, such as houses, shops, office buildings and **tower blocks**.

There may be a school close by and a park where children can play. There may even be a **canal** where, on sunny days, children can go with their parents to see lots of colourful boats.

People can go for walks along the canal. Is there a canal in your area?

A **village** near the coast will be different. There might be **terraced** houses and lots of **bungalows**. There may be a few shops, but no big offices or tower blocks. The streets are usually quiet, except on bank holidays when many people may visit the village.

This street in Cornwall looks out to the sea.

Changes

When you walk around your local area, you may see many changes taking place. You might see new houses being built or an old building being taken down. A new building will have **scaffolding** all around it and you will see it gradually getting bigger.

This house is only partly built. When it is finished, it will be a new home for people to live in.

This road is being repaired. The orange and white cones warn drivers that people are working in the road.

Often old buildings are not taken down completely. Instead they are cleaned up and rebuilt so they can be used in new ways. Old **factories** and warehouses are often turned into flats for people to live in.

There might be small changes in your local area that are not so easy to spot. A new shop might be opening up or a road might be being **repaired**.

A change for the better?

Not everyone is happy when changes happen in a local area. If a new road is to be built, it has to be planned. The local **council** will ask people if they want the change to happen.

Some people will be happy because a new road will make journeys easier and faster. Others will be unhappy because the road building might mean that they have to move from their homes.

This was Twyford Downs in Hampshire just before a new road was built.

This shows the same area in Twyford Downs after the road was built. It doesn't look as pretty now.

Some people will be angry if fields and trees are destroyed to make way for the road. Many will not like the noise that a new road might bring.

Different people like different things in their local area. It is hard to get everyone to agree about how land should be used.

Making it better

Can you think of any ways in which your local area could be made better? There might be a place near you where a playground could be built with ropes, slides and a climbing frame.

Are there changes that other people would like? Older people might like a local park to be tidied up so that they can sit on benches on sunny days.

An adventure playground in your local area would be good for children to play in.

Is there an untidy place in your local area where there should be a rubbish bin like this?

Any local area can be made better by making sure there is no rubbish around. Papers, bottles and empty cans lying in the street look very untidy. It is not safe to pick up other people's rubbish, but you can make sure that you do not drop any yourself.

Activities

- Draw a picture of the street or road where you live. Show the houses and other things that make your street an interesting place.
- Make a list of all the people who visit your street to do important jobs. As well as people who deliver milk and letters, there will be others like the people who collect the rubbish.

Does your street look like this?

Your local area could be brightened up by planting some trees or flowers.

- Talk with your teacher about how your local area could be made better. Look on a map of the area around your school. You might find places where traffic could be slowed down to make the area safer.

- Think about how your local area looks in different seasons of the year. Is there a place near your school where flowers could be planted to cheer everyone up?

Find out for yourself

Websites

You might want to see how your map compares to a real map. Use these websites to find a map of the place where you live. You will need to type in the name of your street and the town or **village** where you live.

- www.multimap.com
- www.ordnancesurvey.gov.uk

You could ask any adult that you know, who has lived in your area for a long time, if it has changed. They might have some photos of how it used to be.

Books

In your neighbourhood: In the street, Franklin Watts, 2001

What was it like in the past? In the street, Louise and Richard Spilsbury, Heinemann Library, 2002

Glossary

bungalow a house with no upstairs rooms

cable a group of wires that carry electricity under the ground

canal a kind of river that has been built by people

council a group of people who plan and run services in their local area

factory a building where things are made using machines

material what something is made of, for example, wood

pavement the part at each side of a street for people to walk along safely

recycling using waste materials, such as old newspapers or glass bottles, to make new materials

repair to fix something

scaffolding a metal and wood frame used by people who build houses

semi-detached two houses that are joined together

terraced a row of houses all joined together

tower block a tall building in which people live in flats

vehicle something that moves and carries things, such as a car or a van

village a group of houses and other buildings in the country

zebra crossing a safe place to cross a street that is marked by black and white stripes on the road and flashing lights on black and white striped poles

Index

Titles in the *What is it like now...?* series include:

Hardback   0 431 15000 1

Hardback   0 431 15002 8

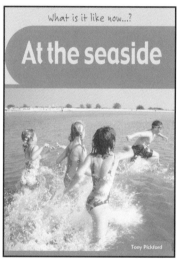

Hardback   0 431 15003 6

Hardback   0 431 15004 4

Hardback   0 431 15001 X

Find out about the other titles in this series on our website www.heinemann.co.uk/library